Lessons from the Couch

Praise for Lessons from the Couch

"I loved it! I wish I would have read this book 30 years ago! --Hannelore Rundell, Co-Founder Montessori School, Hamberg, NY

"An amazingly gifted person and writer. You are an educator at your own expense. I give it an A+! --Joyce Jerome, Executive Assistant, MIHP and TriPLAYnar Technology, Inc.

"All women, at some point in their lives, begin to see the puzzle that is life come together. However, none of us get there without a lot of help from our parents, mentors, friends and spouses. Lessons from the Couch *are the special gifts that ease the journey."* --Cindy Graves, Marketing Director, Macomb Community College

"A little book with a huge message. Good for any age reader. Read it for a NEWSTART. It will change your life." --C. R. Rundell, Retired GM Executive

"Better than The Notebook! Lessons From the Couch *inspired me to reflect upon my life and relationships. I look forward to applying these valuable lessons and enhancing those relationships to their optimum potential."* --Kathleen Butcher, PTA, CSCS

"I read it in one sitting! I love how there are practical lessons and suggestions that everyone can benefit from, no matter how crazed or sane their life is." --Rebecca Tamm, Massage Therapist

"What a blessing!...I was moved to tears. I learned so much. You have brought healing, hope and laughter to me through your words. LOVED IT!" --Monica Myers

"In the pages of Lessons from a Couch, *Sherry manages to skillfully intertwine courageous vulnerability and inspirational teaching. The reader will inevitably find something to identify with and, if willing to give themselves permission to apply wisdom of her experience and most of all God's Word, can improve the quality of their life significantly."* --Rev. Laura Fluke, PTA

"Lessons from the Couch *is a wonderful gift.* Couch Tips *are an easy reference. Thank you and Thank God for sharing this path."* --Debra Moore

"Reading this book I feel like I am sitting on the same couch learning valuable life awakening lessons." --Carl Rundell, Management Consultant

"Sherry speaks from the heart...her words echo the thoughts of the most talented women among us. "Couch" gives a voice to the innermost voice of women everywhere and from every background." --Carol Plisner

Lessons from the Couch

Sherry McLaughlin

First Edition

ML Publishing, Warren, Michigan

Lessons from the Couch

Sherry McLaughlin

Published by:

ML Publishing
Warren, MI 48092, USA

Contents

About the Author

Sherry McLaughlin is the founder of the Michigan Institute for Human Performance, Inc. (MIHP) and TriPLAYnar Technology, Inc., headquartered in Southeastern Michigan. She is also married, a mother of a 12-year old autistic boy, a physical therapist, professional speaker and corporate consultant.

A 1990 graduate of Andrews University, Sherry has practiced in out-patient orthopedic rehabilitation clinics in Southeastern Michigan for over 15 years. She has also served as an adjunct faculty member for Macomb Community College since 1993, instructing courses in Musculoskeletal Physical Therapy and Kinesiology for the physical therapist assistant. She is an orthopedic certified specialist and a certified strength and conditioning specialist.

In 1998, she founded the Michigan Institute for Human Performance (MIHP), a consulting and training company specializing in injury prevention, sport-specific conditioning and orthopedic rehabilitation. She has developed several seminars including The Missing Link, Optimal Athletic Conditioning, Hard Core Training, Optimal Golf and BackTalk, a back injury prevention program that is currently being utilized in several General Motors, Delphi, Sears and Northrop Grummon facilities in the United States. She has served as a consultant to USA Michigan Volleyball and the Detroit Vipers Hockey Organization. She is also the editor of *Synergy*, a bi-monthly newsletter of the MIHP Think Tank, which is currently circulated to health care and fitness professionals nationwide.

Sherry is known by her students, peers and seminar participants as a thought leader in biomechanics through her insightful methods in orthopedic rehabilitation, injury prevention and sports-specific conditioning. She is prolific in her ideas for innovative techniques and has captured them in workbooks, videos and articles that she produces to support her practice and teachings.

Though she has authored several textbooks on biomechanics, musculoskeletal physical therapy and exercise prescription, **Lessons from the Couch** is her first work of this type.

She currently resides with her husband, son and two cousins in Birmingham, MI.

To my husband,
whose honesty and courage
inspired the writing of this book.
I thank the Lord for every day
I get to spend with you.

Preface

I am a 37-year old, happily married, business owner and a mother of a beautiful boy. I was born into a normal family with parents who stayed married and all of my siblings still communicate with me regularly. People have described me as inspiring, positive, a go-getter and a leader. I pray every day. I live in a nice neighborhood, in a nice Midwest town. I drive a vehicle that is less than 3 years old and I have a nice pair of rollerblades and a great mountain bike. By all standards, my life is good—no, it's great.

If you would have told me 2 years ago that I would be sitting on a couch, sharing my deepest thoughts and fears with someone who was paid to listen to me…I would have said you were crazy.

Turns out, I'm the crazy one.

Well, not crazy, according to my hired listener. Just human dealing with life's challenges. Apparently, life beats down even the best of us, sometimes without us even knowing it. She once said to me, "Women who appear to have it all together one day realize that it would be a scary thing for people to know what they really feel inside."

So, there I was. Sitting on her couch, wondering what on earth I could learn from this experience. After all, if all I needed to do was talk, why did I need her? I spoke all day with co-workers, clients, friends and family. Just ask my husband, being short on words has never been my problem.

Though the couch didn't have wheels, I was in for the ride of my life. Perhaps one of the best rides I've ever taken. And that is what this book is about.

How a normal person with a normal life encountered an amazing person with a great couch...and life after that has been nothing short of extraordinary.

Here are the lessons I've learned...

Sherry McLaughlin
Birmingham, MI
2005

Chapter 1

Light a Candle

Come to me, all who are weary and burdened, and I will give you rest. Take my yoke upon you and learn from me, for I am gentle and humble in heart, and you will find rest for your souls. For my yoke is easy and my burden is light.
Matthew 11:28-30 (NIV)

I walked into her office, which resembled a living room right out of the pages of a Pottery Barn catalog. After the normal greeting, she asked me the open-ended question, "How are you doing?"

It was as if my mouth all of a sudden got diarrhea. My introductory monologue was comprised of stories of my day, a sleepless night, a desk load of work, a messy house and a laundry pile that meant the family was about to run out of clean underwear.

When I took a moment to breathe, she gently smiled at me and said, "Are you willing to try something?"

I said, "Sure."

She walked out of the room and came back with a cup of hot tea. Placing a candle in front of me, she said, "Light the candle. Here is a pen and a sticky note. I am going to walk out of the room for a couple of minutes. Try to relax and clear your mind. If something tries to invade your thoughts, write it down."

I was mildly amused. My first thought was, "I'm paying a lot of money...you better come back in a couple of minutes!" But, I was also tired enough to just go along with the process. And with that...she was gone.

Holding the cup of tea, I looked around the room. Weird. Haven't done this in a while. I tried to clear my head. Instead, thoughts of things I needed to get done that day jumped into my brain. I could have balanced my checkbook in this time, made a few phone calls…um…concentrate. Breathe. Write. Breathe. Relax.

Before I knew it, I was mesmerized by the flickering flame. My mind began to clear. The tightness in my chest went away (Funny, I didn't know my chest was feeling tight until it went away). So, this is what it's like to unwind. Breathing was easier. Thinking was easier. The laundry pile in my head even seemed to disappear.

"How are you feeling now?" she asked as she re-entered the room.

Like I want to live here forever, I thought.

"That was 10-minutes."

Really.

Before we continued, we bowed our heads in prayer and it was then I knew I had landed in the right place. Instead of praying for strength and courage, she prayed that I would know that it was OK to admit I was tired and frustrated and overwhelmed. She prayed that I would allow myself to take comfort in the promises of the Bible, and know that real rest came when I let God carry my burdens and gave myself permission to rest.

Your strength will come from settling down in complete dependence on me.
Isaiah 30:15 (The Message)

She said I needed to give myself permission to take care of me. "What happens when you get burned out? How will you juggle your life then?" she asked. She pulled out a small piece of paper and jotted something down. It was my guide to a better life:

N – Nutrition

E – Exercise

W – Water

S – Sunshine

T – Temperance (old word for balance)

A – Air

R – Rest

T – Trust in God

"Make sure you experience these things daily. If you think your life is good now, imagine what it can be when you get some balance," she added. 8 steps to a better life—now that I could tackle.

The session ended with her taking the sticky note I had dumped my thoughts onto and writing Matthew 11:28-30 on the back before putting it in my planner. I see it every day and it brings a comfort and a peace that transcends understanding.

My days now begin with 10-minutes of candlelit conversation with the Lord. My own private vacation before I head out into the crazy world. I have spent a majority of my life worrying about taking care of everything and everybody— and now, someone was looking out for me without expecting anything in return. I had to admit that I didn't really mind it a bit.

A couple of days later, I received an email that I will cherish forever.

Have a peaceful week. Take it one hour at a time. Let God carry you through the day and remember… breathe. Take care. – S

Couch Tip #1

Give yourself permission to:
- Be still and know that He is God (Psalm 46:10)
- Light a candle
- Brain dump on a sticky note
- Breathe deeply
- Get a NEWSTART everyday
- Contemplate the promise of Matthew 11:28

Chapter 2

Set Boundaries

"...And the truth shall set you free."
John 8:32 (NIV)

"So, when did everyone else's time and energy become more important than yours?" I paused before answering that question. I know I take on a lot, but doesn't every working mother and wife? That's just how it works when you are attempting to live the American dream.

You wake up in the morning and plan out your entire day. Right down to the minute. On a good day, you manage to make it into work on time and control your environment. I've often thought that working was a lot easier than staying at home. I'll do battle any day with a pile of paperwork. At least it doesn't whine if I say "no" or feel neglected if I just want to spend a few moments to myself. I generally don't feel guilty if it doesn't get to do something fun or isn't all tidied up by the end of the day. And I certainly don't feel the need to entertain it.

Oh, if only the ones you love could sometimes be like paper. It would be a lot easier to say "no." Instead, they are living, feeling humans that were entrusted to our loving care and we naturally want to give them the best.

"You are entitled to say how you feel and ask for what you need," she said. "Setting boundaries on your time will allow you to be the person God intended you to be. You will be a better wife, mother and professional if you empower yourself to set boundaries. Are you ready to get to work?"

I knew at this point I had officially been admitted into Life Coaching Boot Camp. "Your assignment is to set boundaries at home. Don't let anyone manipulate you into feeling a certain way. You need to be able to say: When you (blank), I feel (blank) and what I need from you is (blank)."

Oh, crap.

I am not a martyr—or at least I have never thought of myself as one. I had often given in to demands on my time usually because I knew I could handle it and I would rather handle it than have to confront someone on an issue or ask someone else to take care of it. This was not going to be easy.

Why was it so hard for me to confront someone? Was I lying to them? No. Was I cheating them? No. I realized for years I had engaged in my own type of deception—not revealing the whole truth by not saying what I really felt. That was the reason for my "time drain". I had put myself in bondage by withholding the truth.

So, I took a deep breath, walked into the

house and got to work on my assignment. That night, I honestly told my husband how I felt, what I needed to do and what I needed from him. His first comment was, "Wow, you have one session with your coach and all of a sudden you are a tough girl." After the shock had passed, he pulled me aside, kissed me and said, "I'm glad you are setting boundaries, even with me. Go do what you need to do. I'll see you when you get back. Come back refreshed." (This stuff actually works!) The evening culminated in quality time spent with my family. My mind was clear, my heart renewed and I was emotionally and mentally 100% present and accounted for.

I would be lying if I said this problem was completely solved that evening. "Boundary problems weren't created overnight and they won't go away overnight either," she said. "Patient endurance will get you through…prayer and being near to the Lord."

I got a taste of what it was like to reclaim a piece of my life and I liked it. I knew I could be patient and endure for that kind of prize.

My lesson for the week: Setting boundaries actually liberates you. Liberates you to do what you need to do, be who you need to be and honor yourself, others and God in the process.

As I read my email the next day, I had to smile in agreement at my coach's advice. She was right again.

The truth in love is when you say "no" when you need to and "yes" to the things you love without resentment. Take care. — S

The truth had set me free.

Couch Tip #2

How to establish healthy boundaries:

- Take care of yourself. You can't give what you yourself don't have.
- Communicate clearly. Say what you mean, mean what you say.
- Use "I choose to" v. "They make me…"
- Pray for clarity.
- Do things that add to your self-worth. This will give you a clear mind to speak freely.
- Choose v. react.

Boundaries are:

- Choosing to respect yourself and others
- Balance
- Honesty
- Setting limits

Boundaries are not:

- Negative
- Confining in a bad way
- Anger-based
- Giving in so that you miss out

Chapter 3

Transforming Value

He who began a good work in you
will be faithful to complete it.
Philippians 1:6 (NIV)

"A moment's insight is sometimes worth a life's experience." That was the quote of the day on my planner page, and it sure seemed apropos. If you would have told me a couple of years ago that I would be experiencing what it was—just now— to truly enjoy life, I would have laughed. I never thought of my life as being hard or draining. Sure it

was always busy—but doable. I've come to realize that just "doing" life doesn't ensure happiness, no matter how upbeat and positive one might be.

"Remember to be real, because that's how you heal," she said. Knowing what I know now, I see just how many in this world need to heal. Not just the ones who are obviously hurting, but even more so the ones who always seem to be OK – like me. That being said, I was finding this transformation a bit challenging. Imagine going through life thinking you're doing it right, only to realize the little compromises you've made along the way in communicating your feelings and letting go of your time and energy have turned into the big hurdle you now have to jump—a hard pill to swallow for an overachieving perfectionist.

My lesson for the week was this: The process of transformation had to begin with me realizing my true worth. Worth and value are determined by the one who makes the purchase. One might look at a car and see that it is worth $40,000, while another might look at the same vehicle with the same price tag and think it an outlandish price. The fact of the matter is this: the whole idea of worth is entirely subjective.

It is one thing when we buy a product and it turns out to be a "lemon". We feel deceived and cheated because the product didn't live up to it's advertising. It is quite another when God purchased us with his life...and He KNEW He was buying a lemon. He knew He was buying broken lives and hearts, desperation and sin. He paid the highest price and He purchased us with joy in His heart.

Aren't two sparrows sold for only a penny? But your Father knows when any one of them falls to the ground. Even the hairs on your head are counted. So don't be afraid! You are worth much more than many sparrows.
Matthew 10:29-31 (CEV)

It was once said, "God would rather go to hell for you than to live in heaven without you." So, who are we to tell the Lord of the Universe what we are worth? His actions **prove** that we are worthy in His eyes.

The insight that was handed to me that week was definitely worth a life's experience. The value of promised solitude; the value of an hour to bend the ear of an unbiased, compassionate, God-fearing person; the warmth of a small candle and the weight that can be lifted when you care enough about yourself and others to just say no— without the need to explain.

Perhaps, the best lesson of all is that when you truly understand your worth, you can ask for that in time, money, emotion and faith without having to look away, understanding that honestly sharing who you are adds value to someone else's life. I realized my worth isn't wrapped up in what I say or what I do. Rather, regardless of what I accomplish, my value has already been determined by a loving God—who saw it fit to concern Himself with my life.

My coach added: *And He promises to carry us through. He brings us to and through life's lessons. Philippians 1:6 is for you today. He does the completing, so give yourself permission to rest and reflect and relax. Take care.* — S

Couch Tip #3

In the time of transformation:

- Reflect on the value that has been placed on you
- Be patient – the Lord is working on you and He will complete it in His time
- Remember the promise of Matthew 10:29-31
- Act to reflect your value

Chapter 4

Couch Dependent

Do not be anxious about anything,
but in everything, by prayer and petition,
with thanksgiving, present your requests to God.
And the peace of God,
which transcends all understanding,
will guard your hearts and your minds in Christ Jesus.
--Philippians 4: 6,7 (NIV)

Imagine growing up without ever having tasted ice cream. You wouldn't crave it on a hot summer day or after eating lasagna. Your life without ice cream would be just fine. People might talk about how good it is, but their statements wouldn't faze you. "What's the big deal?" you ask.

Then one day, someone shares some with you. Not the cheap corner store stuff, but rather the gourmet, make-it-your-way, mouth-watering, richly flavored kind with creative names. You savor the delectable concoction in your mouth and wonder how you ever lived without it.

I use the analogy of ice cream because I was, am and always will be an ice cream lover. In fact, my very first job was at a Baskin Robbins scooping ice cream for a wage of $1.70 an hour. It took me all summer to save up enough to buy a soccer ball. That was the bad news. The good news is that I got to taste all 31 flavors, multiple times. Pure heaven.

A few weeks into this coaching process, I began to realize I had stumbled onto the adult version of ice cream. The feeling of renewal that I got from sitting in a room talking to an adult, who was not emotionally or financially tied to my life, gave me such a rush that I found myself in a weird state of addiction. The chance to vent to someone who on so many levels "got me"—and was able to offer me sound advice and encouragement without judgment was something, I realized, I had not had in a while. Maybe ever.

On one level, I had never felt so good. On another, I didn't seem to know who I was anymore. I sat down and emailed my coach:

It seems like I've jumped a bunch of hurdles and in many ways have felt more periods of relief. So, I can't put my finger on why I'm feeling so discombobulated. Before all this, I felt sharp, or maybe what I thought was sharp. Now, for the first time in a long time I find myself in the strange territory of feeling unsure of myself—I don't even know if that is a good description. It's like I have a cloud in my head or something. I don't know if its because I'm letting my guard down for the first time in weeks; or if its because I'm having to consciously change my reaction to many things as I work on setting boundaries; or if I've been "on" for so long (like a couple of years) that now that I've given myself permission to relax and reflect it is just so foreign that I don't know what to do with it...or maybe I'm just PMS-ing.

I also have never really been dependent on anybody to the degree that I feel dependent on you right now. That is probably the worst thing...no offense. But I have more than once found myself thinking...Thursday at one. Just make it to Thursday at one.

I have never had a difficult time making friends. On the contrary, I usually had no problems connecting with someone. My strength has always been on the giving end of things. I am not a great receiver—but that is a whole other topic. The point is, I found myself in a weird situation. It was as if I had made a new friend, only I wasn't really allowed to know anything about her. Our conversations were largely one-sided, concerning me and my life. I was eternally grateful for our time together, but felt like I wasn't allowed to reciprocate. And yet, I needed her. This was a strange place for me to be, indeed.

I figured I was walking down the wrong path with this dependence thing. But then again, how could something so wrong feel so right?

I should not have ever doubted that an answer was just around the corner. She smiled at me and said, "I need you to stop trying to take care of me. This hour is about you, not me. God is the one leading you and guiding you into the truth that will continue to set you free. I would encourage you to give yourself permission to 'adjust'. There is a lot that you are learning and your body, mind and emotions are all adjusting to change. Try to reframe your dependence on me to dependence on God. You are capable and will be fine through this process. Relax and resist the temptation to have it all figured out." That week, I got my next assignment:

Try something new: Have your journaling experience this week be in the form of letters to God. His email is always on and He never misses a beat. His answers are always on time, right when we need Him. He is always there. Take care. – S

Couch Tip #4

It's OK to depend on someone
every now and then.
Receive it gracefully and thank them for it.
Though it might feel one-sided, it probably isn't.
The benefit of an honest relationship
goes both ways.

Chapter 5

Writing God

"...I know whom I have believed, and am convinced that
He is able to guard what I have entrusted to Him
for that day."
--2 Timothy 1:12 (NIV)

God,

I'm doing this because I was told to. Funny, I've spoken to You practically all of my life, so I'm wondering why it feels odd to be writing You now. Regardless, I was instructed to do so by someone who walks daily with You and so far, her advice has been right on.

I guess the good thing is that I don't really have to catch You up on what has been going on in my life. That's one great thing about having an all knowing, all seeing Friend. That being said, You probably knew all along that I would end up in this place. Maybe that's why I'm here…so that today, I would be taking the time to talk to You. Really talk.

I remember when I was younger, my faith was so strong that when I came to You with my concerns of the day, I just knew You would take care of things. Like helping me get an A on an exam so my GPA wouldn't drop. It's crazy to think that that was my main concern back then…but it was. I had no problems knowing that a big God like you would concern yourself with a small person like me.

Now, I'm closer to 40. I've accomplished a fair amount. More than ever, I've got people looking to me for guidance: emotionally, financially, morally and spiritually. Somehow, I've found myself in this place where I'm so busy ensuring other people's worth and happiness that I've forgotten about mine.

It has been said that it's lonely at the top. I know what that feels like now. Despite the fact that I am constantly surrounded, I realize that now more than ever, most of the people I come in contact with expect something from me. There is the expectation of leadership, the expectation of companionship, the expectation of strength. I've risen to the occasion and done so with poise, so much so that I've forgotten what it was like to feel like someone was looking out for me.

Well, I got that reminder—just in time. You sent me to a place where I can speak freely without judgment—a place where I am allowed to vent my fears, frustrations and hopes without offending anyone or marring my image or affecting my business. Best of all, You sent me to someone who has reminded me of just how big You are and how concerned You are with my life.

As I look back on the past couple of years, there have been many times I have been reminded of your existence. It's funny how often I've prayed that Your will be done in my life, only to quickly add some instructions on how I would like to see it happen. Clearly, you have misplaced those instructions. Thank God (can You thank

Yourself?) that You did.

I pride myself on being a big dreamer, but I realize I can't hold a candle to the life plan You have for me. I see it now. Your business plan is way better than mine. It is a weird dichotomy. The stronger and wiser I get, the more dependent I am on You. That appears to be the lesson of the week for me: that it's OK to say I need some help. You had to beat me over the head and trip me up a couple of times, but these earthly bruises will be worth getting to spend an eternity in heaven.

Someone recently asked me if I've ever heard your voice. I'm not sure I have, but without a doubt I've felt your presence. Thank You for hearing me. Thank You for answering.

I'll talk to You again soon, I'm sure. Until then, know that I love You.

Sherry

Couch Tip #5

Put your trust in God.
His email is always on and
He never misses a beat.
He is always there—right when we need him.
And His answers are always on time.

Chapter 6

Good 'n Guilty

*"And this is my prayer: that your love may abound more
and more in knowledge and depth of insight, so that you
may be able to discern what is best and
may be pure and blameless..."*
--Philippians 1:9,10 (NIV)

Guilty pleasures. We often associate those
two words with something decadent, like Godiva
chocolates, milkshakes or Fettuccini Alfredo. Or
ice cream. Funny thing is, I seldom feel guilty

about eating that stuff. I figure if I eat it, I can always make up for it by running around the block or doing 100 jumping jacks or something.

I do feel guilty a lot, though. Like when I take off to go rollerblading when everyone is home, or if I go out with the girls for an evening or if I just want to jump in bed and go right to sleep. My happiness usually comes second.

I realize this is self-imposed, but it is there just the same. I don't think I'm much different than your average working mom in this situation. Working mom. That's a recipe for guilt right there.

Not guilty enough? Then just be successful at your job. You will earn more responsibility and you will want to stay there longer. Life at work is easier because there are clear expectations and goals and you can control it. When you are successful at what you do, you might be exhausted—but the affirmation that you are making a difference is a pretty good reward.

Now, of course, at home you are making

a difference. But in the home arena, you are entrusted with a motley crew of individuals that you aren't allowed to fire and your "office" often resembles a war zone. Need an example? Just try to herd a group of 5 into the car to grab a bite to eat. Or try to make that laundry pile disappear by doing a little bit every day. And if you were really going to do your job right, you would just keep the vacuum cleaner running 24/7. You love them to death—and that is the dilemma. Loving them is sometimes like running on sand against a rough wind. Maybe you're having fun, but you are getting nowhere fast. Which leads me to the question, "How can something so right, feel so wrong?"

"Guilt can be a good thing, you know," she said.

Huh?

"Just as a guideline, when it comes to your personality, if you are feeling guilty about what you said or did, you are probably doing the right thing," she explained.

Really. Well, that was great news to me. I decided to put it to the test:

1. Scheduled a massage and facial (guilty—but my coach made me do it)

2. Went to a seminar on a weekend (guilty)

3. Played paddle tennis with some friends on a weekend (guilty)

4. Came home after paddle tennis to find the house cleaned by husband and son (really guilty—but happy it got done)

5. Fell asleep at 10 p.m. (guilty)

6. Took an entire day off of work—despite the fact that I had tons to do (major guilt)

7. Ate a brownie (not guilty)

Oh, boy. I think she was right again.

Couch Tip #6

If you feel guilty about doing
something for yourself—
Do it anyway.
You'll get over the guilt, and you'll thank
yourself in the morning.

Chapter 7

Playing catch...or not

And when they bring you before the
synagogues and the rulers and the authorities,
do not be anxious about how you
should defend yourself or what you should say,
for the Holy Spirit will teach you in that very hour
what you ought to say.
Luke 12:11 (ESV)

"What do you want to work on today?"
she asked. I'm feeling pretty good, I thought. Let's

not do anything hard. Instead, I took a moment to think of the challenges of my week.

I had an important meeting scheduled, one that I knew would require some thick skin on my part, and I was not feeling particularly up to the challenge. Could all of this touchy, feely conversation have made me soft? No. I decided this was the kind of meeting that I usually cowered from. Confrontation was never my strong point. Even if I knew I was right, I would rather bow out, than cause a fight.

"What is the real issue about this meeting?" she asked. I told her that I dreaded going into the room because I knew there were going to be comments made about me that would elicit snickers.

"Just because someone throws you the ball, doesn't mean you have to catch it," she said. I really enjoyed my time with her, but sometimes I swear I felt like I needed a translator—this was one of those times.

"People can say a lot of things," she explained, "Just because they say something doesn't mean you have to respond to it." She went on to say that many times we feel the need to respond to every statement that is thrown our way. When that occurs, we tend to get caught up in a power struggle that can end up in a losing battle.

"Wait until everyone is done talking. Instead of responding after each comment, just take a deep breath. Respond only if they ask you a question."

She instructed me to ask myself two questions as I listened: *What do I feel? And what do I need to say?* Great, I thought. She is going to make me do homework at this meeting! Despite my trepidation at having to try out a new technique during such a stressful situation, my ears were tuned into her instructions. After all, if making it through a meeting could be as easy as waiting for a question, I think I could handle that.

"What if a question is never asked?" I said.

"Then a response must not be necessary," she replied.

Really.

She went on to explain that if I thought they were waiting for a response, I could simply say, "I hear you saying (blank). Now, what is it you need from me?"

"Wait until all the cards are on the table, then react to them. When it is all said and done, you might just find yourself staring at a bunch of harmless cards."

The session ended with us bowing our heads in prayer. She asked the Lord to give me the courage to say what I needed to say and to "go ahead" of me in this meeting. I will admit, I drove a little slower that day—just to make sure He beat me there.

The meeting began and the comments I was dreading came quickly. Some of them stung a bit, probably because I knew they were coming and what the general reaction would be. I just took a deep breath and listened. As the remarks continued, it was at this point that I figured I was being tossed the proverbial ball—and I was choosing not to catch it. I waited to see if there was going to be a question addressed to me and it never came.

When the talking stopped and all the cards were on the table, I looked up amusingly, realizing my coach had been right—again. I took a deep breath, looked them straight in the eye and said, "So, what is it you need from me?"

I think everyone was momentarily stunned. My question seemed to have immediately diffused the situation. (By golly, this stuff really works!) From that point on, the meeting progressed with ease.

I walked out of the room feeling empowered, wishing I had a chance to sit in all of the meetings of my past where I cowered or backtracked from negative or confrontational statements.

"Listen to what you know, instead of what you fear."
                                        —Richard Bach

Apparently, that was my lesson for the week. I rushed home to email my coach. Her response was like a proverbial pat on the back:

Great job! I knew you could do it. – S

Couch Tip #7

When faced with confrontational conversation:

- Listen attentively until all the cards are on the table
- Use reflective listening "Feels like…sounds like"
- Don't get caught up in a power struggle
- Don't feel the need to answer until a question is asked
- Then ask, "What is it you need from me?"

Chapter 8

Tough Enough

*It is God who arms me with strength
and makes my way perfect.*
--Psalm 18:32 (NIV)

People that know me would never call me
a wimp. I have done battle on many an athletic
field, received bumps and bruises and doled out
my share of pain. In fact, I'm sort of known for
being scrappy. You know, not necessarily skilled
at any one particular sport, but athletic enough
to throw my body around in some coordinated

fashion that it creates the illusion that I know what I'm doing. I also appear to be made of rubber. Knock me down, and I'll bounce back up. People think its because I'm tough—I think its because my legs are so short that it isn't that far of a fall. But, I digress.

I'm also mentally tough. Give me a complicated problem and I will think about it until my head hurts. My husband once told me a story of a Russian chess champ who thought so hard that his brain imploded. I can sort of picture what that might feel like—but I'm hoping that's an urban legend.

Starting a business toughened me up emotionally. Lets face it. Crying in the boardroom isn't necessarily acceptable—and it won't get you any funding. When push comes to shove in business, I have learned to set my jaw, respectfully stand my ground and weather the storm. I was about to learn how all of this toughness could be mind numbing.

"So how do you feel about that?" she would ask.

"I don't know," would often be my reply.

"Say three words that describe how you feel."

"Umm…" I would manage to stammer something out.

"Those are not feeling words," she would say.

What was going on? I couldn't believe with my advanced education and all of the letters I have after my name, I couldn't come up with the right answers to her question—a simple set of words to describe how I feel.

After a few failed attempts and some long pauses, she stood up and said, "Here. Pick something off of this page." She handed me a piece of paper with the *Feeling Wheel* on it.

Oh, my gosh. I know she didn't just hand me a cheat sheet of words to get me through this task. Valedictorians don't need cheat sheets. Ouch.

"Women who appear to have it all together one day realize that it would be a scary thing for people to know what they really feel inside," she said. "You have to be tough in business, you have to be brave when you go up and speak. You have to have it all together all of the time."

She went on to explain how women with really busy lives rarely stop long enough to allow their emotions to register. Sometimes we just need to be still and feel what we feel. "It's only feelings," she said. "It's OK to allow yourself to feel something, without having to explain or make sense of why you are feeling the way you feel. That's how you free yourself."

As her words sunk in, I realized how often I had buried emotions that would be deemed as weak. Fear. Sadness. Exhaustion. When my life called for these emotions to take place, I simply convinced myself that life really wasn't all that bad. Get over it and move on. Apparently, my attempts to get over stuff—had just buried those things even deeper.

"It's a vulnerable place to be," she said gently. "But remember, where we are weak, He is strong. God knows what you are going through and He can handle it." She reminded me of the importance of being real with myself.

It is a lesson that would not come easily for me. Being vulnerable had never been one of my strong points. But slowing down sounded pretty attractive at this point, and if it meant that I might feel something uncomfortable along the way, then so be it. At least my Partner on this journey was good at picking up the slack.

It was once said, "There are two things I've learned: There is a God. And I am not Him." One with God is the majority. That thought alone ought to give us courage to face our feelings.

I have since allowed myself to be still enough to acknowledge what I really feel: at the end of a long day, in rush hour traffic, standing in front of my father's grave…It was during those moments that the lesson of the week became clear: If I let God be God, then I could be free to be me. And I liked how that felt.

I'm still made of rubber, but thanks to my coach's sound advice, the plumbing in my eyes seems to work much better now. And as I head out the door each morning, I am reminded of a sign I recently saw taped to a friend's shower door:

Good morning, this is GOD.
I will be handling all of your problems today.
I will not need your help.
So, have a good day.

Ah, yes…free to be me.

Couch Tip #8

Give yourself permission to be still—and feel.
It might make you feel vulnerable.
But remember, where we are weak, He is strong.
Letting God be God frees you up to be you.

Chapter 9

The First Conversation of the Rest of Your Life

*"Trust in the LORD with all your heart
and lean not on your own understanding."*
Proverbs 3:5 (NIV)

I am a pretty perceptive person and I love to solve puzzles. I always have. I remember spending hours a day doing crossword puzzles and word searches. Encyclopedia Brown was my childhood hero. (Now you know why I didn't get asked out until I was 17). But I was about to find out that my need to always guess the answers wasn't a good thing.

"What is on your mind today?" she asked.

Well, there was this upcoming business trip. A chance for me to get away from the hustle and bustle of my everyday world. It had been a particularly trying month and I was looking forward to the chance at a solo departure—and some sleep.

Small problem. My husband was expecting to come with me. This was by no means an outlandish request. After all, it had been almost a year since we'd gotten away together and Lord knows we both needed to get away. "What do I say to that?" I asked.

"I'm wondering what you would say to him right now if you knew you wouldn't hurt his feelings," she replied.

Uh, oh. I felt an assignment coming on. "Are you going to make me tell him?" I asked.

"No. But if you can't say what you really want to say here, then when will you say it?"

Good point. Maybe I'll just say we can't afford the ticket. Or I'll rationalize that the trip is too short, and we wouldn't have much time to do anything together.

"That's manipulative," she said.

Ouch.

"The problem is, I know what his reaction is going to be. He is going to be hurt and disappointed."

"How do you know?" she asked.

"I just know." I replied. It's not like I just met him yesterday. Immediately after I said it, I knew that wasn't going to be an acceptable answer.

"You need to take life one conversation at a time. Don't try to guess what the other person is going to say. And don't form your words based on what you think the other person is going to say," she said.

This was going to take some work. In the business world, one is often taught what to say and how to say it. Some learn by experience. For the rest of us, there are a plethora of books aimed at schooling us in the art of conversation: *How to Make People Like You in 90 Seconds or Less.* Or how about *How to Use Power Phrases to Say What You Need and Get What You Want* or *The Pocket Guide to Successful Small Talk: How to Talk to Anyone, Anywhere, Anytime about Anything.* Then there's my personal favorite, *What to Say When You Talk to Yourself.* Really. The resources are endless and it seems as though we have overeducated ourselves right into a corner.

Despite what the abundance of resources said, my coach had only one piece of advice...just say it. Say what you mean and mean what you say. Obviously, a novel concept.

I took her advice. Over dinner that night, I took a deep breath and told my husband about my need for a solo trip. He smiled at the anxious look on my face and said, "I think it's a good idea.

Then you can get some sleep." He continued, "I'm glad you told me how you really feel. When you don't tell me everything, I feel like you don't trust me and that hurts more than anything you could possibly say." I have been with this man for 18 years and even I had guessed this ending wrong.

I thought about all of the times I had skirted around issues to soften the blow or just plain avoided saying anything at all. Oh, how I had wasted time and energy on needless anxiety and the resulting resentment I felt when I didn't just come out and say what I meant.

You never know what gift you could have given,
just by being the real you.

--Dr. Joseph Dremer

There is strength in honesty, after all. You can't argue with the truth—nor do you need to. Being honest puts an end to chaos and power struggles and being honest builds a solid foundation for relationships.

I reported the results to my coach and her reply said it all…

Praise God. What a wonderful testimony of the healing process in motion. Remember, being real gives the other person permission to do the same. Take care. – S

Couch Tip #9

Take life one conversation at a time.

Don't plan your statements on what you
think the other person might say.

Being real gives the other person
permission to be the same.

Chapter 10

Just Receiving

Your beauty should not come from outward adornment…
instead, it should be that of your inner self,
the unfading beauty of a gentle and quiet spirit,
which is of great worth in God's sight.
I Peter 3:3,4 (NIV)

"Have you had real conversations this week?" she asked. That was a whopper of an opening question.

"I think so," I replied, as I surveyed the

past several days worth of conversations.

"Who would you say you have the hardest time being real with?" she asked.

Gotta love that kind of persistence. I thought for a moment and then answered, "Believe it or not, I would have to say my husband."

I don't know if it was a surprise to her, but as soon as the words left my mouth, I was a bit puzzled. My husband and I met over 18 years ago – and we have been inseparable since. A whirlwind of a love story, we were engaged after two and a half months. If it had not been for the stipulation imposed by my parents that we wait until I had obtained my degree, we probably would have gotten married quickly. Instead, we honored their wishes and we were married two and a half years later, 3 weeks after I graduated with my Master's Degree.

I am one of the lucky ones. I married a man who still looks me square in the eye and tells me how beautiful and wonderful I am—multiple times a day. I am constantly reminded of how much I mean to him – even after all of these years. It isn't unusual to have a majority of our date night dinner conversations revolve around accolades to me.

Ironically, that makes me uncomfortable.

"Why is that?" she asked.

I looked up at the ceiling trying to figure it out. After all, wouldn't all women die to have that kind of daily adoration heaped on them from their husbands? "I guess its because I feel like its overkill – and I really don't know how to respond to it." I said.

She asked me what my usual response is to receiving a compliment. I thought for a moment and replied, "I usually try to downplay it."

She proceeded to pick up a small box. "Let's say this box represents a compliment. It is a gift. Let's say God hands this gift to someone to deliver to you. When you downplay or push away a compliment, it is as if you are denying the gift." And with that, she drop-kicked the box. As it rolled under the table, I was stunned at how harsh the example looked—and even more stunned at my reaction to it.

"What do you think it makes the person who gave you that compliment feel like when you push their compliment away?"

Pause.

"How would you feel if someone took the gift you were trying to hand them and they drop kicked it?"

Well, when you put it that way…

She let that sink in for a moment and then said, "I want you to list 3 words that describe how you would feel if someone did that to you." This stuff was getting hard. I thought for a moment before saying these words: unimportant, dissatisfied, betrayed.

"Hmm," she mused. "What are the opposites of those 3 words?"

Valued. Satisfied. Trusted.

"When you think of those 3 words," she continued, "when or where during your day do you experience those feelings."

Without hesitation, I replied, "At work."

"You are going to hate me," she said.

At this point, I was so intrigued, I don't think I could have hated anything. She took out a piece of paper and drew a diagram:

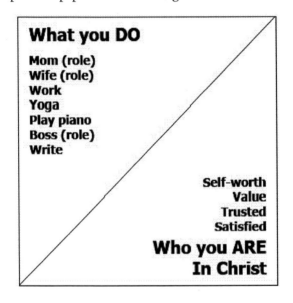

What you DO

Mom (role)
Wife (role)
Work
Yoga
Play piano
Boss (role)
Write

Self-worth
Value
Trusted
Satisfied

Who you ARE
In Christ

"You have placed your value and worth in the wrong half of the box," she explained. "What you do has no bearing on who you are. Your value is not determined by what you accomplish in a day or how successful you are." The next thing she said will stick with me for the rest of my life.

"You are a human-doing.
God intended you to be a human-being."

She then picked a copy of my weekly schedule, which was chock full of appointments and obligations. "This has nothing to do with your worth. You are worthy simply because God said so."

It was then I realized why my conversations with my husband were often uncomfortable for me. His constant accolades did not at all fit in with my picture of value or self-worth. How could I really be what he was saying? The house was a mess, I seldom got a meal on the table, I was often exhausted, and not the fun-loving girl he fell in love with. It was difficult for me to receive those compliments because frankly, I didn't believe them.

Her illustrations that day hit me at the core. I realized how many gifts I had drop kicked in the past, and I vowed then and there that I would receive them graciously from here on out—simply because God said I was worthy.

My coach then wrote I Peter 3:3,4 on my piece of paper. I copied it into my planner so that I see it everyday as a reminder of my worth.

This is where most of your healing will happen in simply giving yourself permission to receive. It is like works verses grace and faith. You need both to be balanced. Take care. — S

Couch Tip #10

If you are having a hard time just receiving:

- Remember to separate out what you do from who you are in Christ. You are worthy because He says you are.
- Think about the promise of I Peter 3:3,4
- Receive compliments with a simple smile and "thank you." It is a gift from God. Resist the temptation to have to return the compliment.

Chapter 11

Empty Buckets

You have looked deep into my heart, LORD,
and you know all about me.
--Psalm 139:1 (NIV)

"So how does that happen?" I asked. "How does one grow up in a loving, nurturing home and end up with a skewed perception of self-worth?"

She smiled at me gently and said, "You'll figure it out."

At this point, I wanted to jump out of my skin. I had no problems solving puzzles on a daily basis. This puzzle had me stumped and my coach seemed to have the answer—only she wasn't going to give it away.

"Are you ready to do some work?" she asked. I was on to her now. Whenever she asked me this question, things were going to get a bit rough. "Sure," I answered bravely. Bring it on.

She handed me a piece of paper entitled *The Basic Emotional Needs of a Child*. Apparently, during the first seven years of a child's life, the brain is dependent on certain input to function properly. Things that were listed were:

1.   To be loved unconditionally
2.   Acceptance – to be received, to be heard, to be included, to be considered important
3.   Affirmation – words of encouragement
4.   Support – supply strength and encouragement to achieve

5.   Trust – to be able to rely on a primary care-giver

6.   Knowledge – receive knowledge and instruction

7.   Safe & Nurturing Touch – without fear of pain or invasion

8.   Direction – training for self-government (boundaries)

9.   Participation – active caring and time devoted to child

10.   Security – consistent, peaceful, happy environment to grow

11.   Wings of Individuality – freedom at the appropriate age

She asked me to rate both my mother and father on a scale of 1-9 on each of these items. 1 if they never provided me these things and 9 if they were perfect at it.

As I went down the list, I thought back to my childhood. By all standards, I was raised in the perfect family environment. The 2nd of 4 children,

I grew up with a strong sense of family security and love.

My parents lived a love story themselves. They immigrated to the United States from the Philippines shortly after they were married, eternally grateful for the chance at a new life in the Land of the Free. My mother is an extremely loving person – the family glue. As my father was busy working to support the family and start several private practices, she took on a majority of the child-rearing. She nurtured us, taught us, gave us opportunities and challenged us on many levels. We were often reminded of how fortunate we were to be born in this country. I remember my mother scolding us if we were slow to act on her instruction, "This is America and in America you must move fast!" She would tell us that opportunities came and went and if we didn't jump up and take them, it would be our loss.

I lived and died by this principle. The support and encouragement I got from my parents gave me the confidence to attempt anything I wanted—and I usually succeeded. So much so that at one point in my childhood, all I had to say was that I wanted to play a particular musical instrument—and before I knew it, that instrument was mine, complete with lessons. By the age of 14, I played 12 instruments, my days filled with practicing, instruction and performing. That is a story in itself.

My parents set the bar on their expectations of us, and we would meet that bar without hesitation. Not just to please them, but because it was instilled so deeply in us that we could. And I was the one child that begged them to keep pushing that bar a little higher so I could learn even more.

As my eyes scanned the list, they rested on the word "affirmation." I paused. I didn't recall many times where my parents openly complimented me for what I did. I didn't expect it, really. It is a typical trait of Asian families to invest a lot in their children—the best education and opportunities to expand their knowledge and experience. It is a typical trait of an Asian child to simply rise to the challenge—not because a compliment would be received, but because it was simply what you did.

That being said, I wasn't sure at first how to score the "affirmation" line.

"How did you know when you did a good thing?" she asked.

"I'm not sure. I just knew," I replied.

"Did they give you a high-five or pat you on the back? Did they give you a 'thumbs up' sign? How did you know?"

I paused and then said, "I usually heard them telling someone else. That's how I knew I had made them happy."

"So, you grew up not knowing how to receive a compliment that was given to you face to face." As I let this sink in, she continued. "This is not a judgment on your parents. They clearly raised you in a loving home. They did the best with what they had. The point is that during your childhood, you form file folders in your head for each of these 11 traits. If one isn't formed, then you have no place to file away the things that are coming at you."

Things were becoming clear to me now.

"What are you feeling?" she asked. She handed me a list of words and told me to jot down the words that described what I was feeling as I looked at the list of emotional needs and how they were fulfilled during my childhood. I wrote: Thoughtful, Thankful, Worthwhile, Hopeful.

She asked me to explain and I replied, "I am thankful for the loving home that I was raised in, for the support and encouragement my parents gave me while I was growing up." I went onto explain how worthwhile this assignment had been. I felt like I finally had the answers to why I couldn't just receive without feeling the need to return the favor, gift or compliment. And that gave me hope.

"Have I ever told you the story about the buckets?" she asked. I smiled. Couldn't wait to hear this one. "God has this picture of who He intends you to be. Imagine you standing with all of these buckets surrounding you. Your parents filled many of those buckets, some to overflowing. But there are these buckets that maybe didn't get any water in them. Look at this list," she said as I surveyed the list I had ranked earlier. "God saw that there were some empty buckets that needed to be filled to make you the person He intended you to be. He saw that you needed a man to fill the areas of affirmation and participation to pick up where your father left off. He saw that need—those empty buckets—and he sent you your husband."

As the weight of her statement sunk in, I felt a sense of clarity and then a sense of humbleness—the kind of feeling you get when you hike up a mountain and look over the vast expanse of land beneath you. Yelling at the top of your lungs at that point seems inadequate. As you stand there taking in the beauty and the grandeur, you simply stand—in awe. Someone was in control—and He was looking out for me.

I wasn't crazy. The God of the Universe

lead me to this place so that I would learn how intimately He was involved in my life. So involved that He took the time to send me on this journey, with all of its ups and downs, successes and failures, frustrations and defeats. He took the time and energy to see to it that I was brought to a place where my buckets would be filled—right down to the man I would spend the rest of my life with.

"This is as deep as it gets," she said. "Think about how awesome that is. When you realize that God valued you so much that he took the time to concern Himself with your life, you will simply be the person he designed you to be."

I can't describe exactly what I felt at that moment. But when I looked up at my coach, I saw tears in her eyes, and I knew she understood.

All of the confusion and frustration of the past several weeks finally made sense. At times it had felt like I was wandering aimlessly, anxiously looking for what I was supposed to be getting out of all this and where I was supposed to be headed.

This journey started and ended differently than I had planned.

And once again, I thanked God that it did.

Couch Tip #11

God has a plan for who He intended you to be. In order to determine what that plan is:

- Ask. Believe. Listen. Follow.
- Know that things might not always go as you plan. Remember, you asked for His will to be done. His vision is much bigger – and clearer.
- God wants us to be successful here on earth, but more importantly, He wants to save our souls. If we ask that His will be done, He will use various methods to get our attention if He needs to.
- Be still and know that HE is God. He is in control – and He is looking out for you.

Chapter 12

Writing God (again)

The LORD is my shepherd, I shall not be in want. He
makes me lie down in green pastures, he leads me beside
quiet waters, he restores my soul.
--Psalm 23:1-3 (NIV)

God,

I thought I had it all figured out. My life. My
plan. You. I don't know what would possess me to think
that. I should have known your plan was way better—it
always is.

So, forgive me for grumbling along the way. My complaints about being tired or frustrated seem so petty right now. It reminds me of when my dad used to plan family trips. He would have the whole thing scheduled down to the minute. No sleeping in for us—we had things to do and places to see. Often, we would grumble about the structure and the schedule, only to realize that when it was all said and done, we were privy to some pretty great experiences because he chose not to listen to our complaining—and taught us the lessons we needed to learn anyway, simply because he loved us.

This week I've learned so many things about You and Your mercy. I can imagine You looking down at me, running around at the speed of light trying to get everything done by yesterday. I imagine You saw my exhaustion. I bet You tried to stop me—to tell me to slow down and be still in You. I bet You tried it many times, and I was just too busy to listen. Well, You got my attention—and thank God You did.

As I replay the events of the past month and a half, I realize Your hand was in it all along. The times I thought You had forgotten me were really just parts of a journey that I needed to go through to get to this place. Again, Your plan was better than mine.

I once heard someone say that if we could see our life the way You see it, from beginning to end, we would choose to do it like You would—with all of the trials and temptations and sorrows still mixed in. I realize I had gotten so used to being the potter that I had forgotten how to just be the clay. My life was spinning around and You were trying to mold me, and in my stubbornness and "busy"ness, I just kept trying to jump off of the wheel. Thanks for not letting me.

When this whole process started, I asked You "why" so many times. Again, I'm not sure that I've ever heard Your voice—but I got your answer.

Thanks for looking out for me, despite that fact that there are bigger problems and bigger things that require Your attention. I guess that's the great thing about being omnipotent, huh?

I'm sure I will be talking to you again soon. Until then, know that I love You.

Sherry

Couch Tip #12

- God is a personal God. He wants to hear your thoughts.
- Writing God a letter is a method of processing your thoughts and fears – and getting answers to your questions.
- Even if you don't hear his voice, His answers are loud and clear.
- Remember the promise of Psalm 23. He is more than capable of restoring your soul from the crazy life you create.

Epilogue

The Rest of the Story

For all practical purposes, I should have never met my life coach. Certain circumstances landed me in the waiting room of the office that she happened to share with 19 other professionals—I had spoken to her on the phone earlier that day, but I was there on behalf of someone else. As I sat in a chair, furiously typing on my laptop trying to catch up from a day interrupted, I heard her call my name. When I looked up, I had no idea the journey had already begun.

She had come back to the office, after her

day had ended, because she felt God telling her to. She motioned me out into the hallway and said, "Pretty rough day, huh?"

I just leaned up against the wall and nodded.

"Do you want to talk?" she asked.

I shrugged. I didn't think that I really needed to talk...well, maybe I did. I figured I was getting tired and didn't want to work anymore anyway. So, I followed her into her office, we bowed our heads in prayer...and the rest is history.

It would be pompous for me to assume that everyone who picked up this book would receive the healing and comfort that I received by writing it. But, I also think it would be ignorant to believe that at least one person wouldn't. That is why I wrote this book.

If you are feeling overwhelmed, exhausted and unfulfilled, then I hope you heard the message of my story loud and clear. There is a God—a personal God—who is capable of taking your life, remolding it and handing it back to you all fixed up. He created you for a reason and it is up to you to let Him take your life and turn it into something extraordinary. You might be a highly driven, motivated person like myself, but trust me, your dreams can't hold a candle to what He has in store for you.

That's the thing about free will, though. It won't happen unless you ask—really ask, believe and trust that the path you will be led down is the one you want to take.

It has been said that God works in mysterious ways. I believe it now more than ever. As I reflect back on my time with my coach, I realize the transformation that had taken place. Initially, I viewed her as a hired listener. She was sincere and concerned, but she was doing her job. Pretty quickly, I felt drawn to her faith. As she spoke of the power of God and understanding His will, I realized she really believed it. This wasn't just a job for her. She got me, not because some book told her how to get people like me, but rather because she had experienced similar feelings and similar circumstances and God had led her to a better place. She was patient when she had to be. She was direct when she had to be. She was quiet when I needed her to be. But, most importantly, she was real—always real. It wasn't long before my view of her changed from that of a hired listener to a great friend in the Lord. And I mean that in the deepest sense.

I don't know how long we will continue to meet. I once asked her if she saw normal people. She just smiled. I'm not sure she is allowed to answer that one.

I hope I get the chance to repay her, but if I don't I will graciously receive the gift of our time together. We will probably never do lunch or hang out at Starbucks. But she will hold a very special place in my heart—for eternity. I will never forget her. Once a hired listener, then a friend, but bigger than that, she is the one God sent to rescue me from the crazy life I had created.

So, I hope you take the time to seek out the Lord and His plan for your life. There really isn't anything He can't handle and He's got some interesting methods to get your attention. Ask Him. You never know. He might speak to you or send you a sign. Or He might send you someone to help you along the way.

And maybe, just maybe, she might have a great couch.

My Coach's Final Thought...

The process of healing is a journey that many resist. When a brave soul takes that step to trust God, miracles happen. Your journey is one of those miracles. Continue to always give credit to the Miracle Maker and what happens next is indeed bliss! - S

Visit us on-line:

lessonsfromthecouch.com

Appendix
(Other things I wanted to include)

Be Careful With Your Donkey

An old man, a boy and a donkey were going to town. The boy rode on the donkey & the old man walked. As they went along they passed some people who remarked it was a shame the old man was walking & the boy was riding. The man & boy thought maybe the critics were right, so they changed positions.

Later, they passed some people that remarked, "What a shame, he makes that little boy walk." They then decided they both would walk! Soon they passed some more people who thought they were stupid to walk when they had a decent donkey to ride. So, they both rode the donkey.

Now they passed some people that shamed them by saying how awful to put such a load on a poor donkey. The boy & man said they were probably right, so they decided to carry the donkey. As they crossed the bridge, they lost their grip on the animal & he fell into the river and drowned.

The moral of the story?
If you try to please everyone, you might as well...
Kiss your ass good-bye.

Be Careful With Your Donkey
--Author unknown

Attitude
Charles Swindoll

"The longer I live, the more I realize the impact of attitude on life. Attitude, to me is more important than facts. It is more important than the past, than failures, than successes, than what other people think or say or do. It is more important than appearance, giftedness, or skill. It will make or break a company...a church...a home. The remarkable thing is we have a choice everyday regarding the attitude we will embrace for that day. We cannot change our past...we cannot change the fact that people will act a certain way. We cannot change the inevitable. The only thing we can do is play on the one string we have, and that is our attitude...I am convinced that life is 10% what happens to me and 90% how I react to it."

Non-Negotiable Needs

By Drs. Ron and Nancy Rockey

To be loved unconditionally

> Accepted right where I am
>
> Based on the fullness of the giver
>
> Without having to earn or barter

To experience a senses of personal identity

> Seen as the unique person I am
>
> Affirmed and encouraged
>
> Valuable and worthwhile

To know that I am not alone

> I am connected to a unit; people care about me
>
> I belong, I'm like someone
>
> Others even feel the way I do; shared experiences

Note: Drs. Ron and Nancy Rockey also developed the The Basic Emotional Needs of a Child *referred to on pp. 81, 82. Their website:* itsfixable.com.

Life in My Day

A meaningful and slightly rambunctious song
by Newsong
(with my favorite parts bolded)

My cell phone's ringing and I'm running late
The morning traffic's got me time is ticking away
A few more hours is all that I need
Seems that there's just not enough days in the
week

But then it hits me
Time is not the answer
You've given me all the time in the world
All that I need…

[Chorus]
Is a little more life in my day
A little more of Your life
A little more faith
Need a little more life in my day
A little more of Your light to show me the way
If I'm gonna be in this world but not be of it
Lord I need more of You in all that I do
With a little more life in my day

Sometimes I guess I get lost in the race
Trying to make a deadline just to keep up the pace
I can't help feelin' I'm always behind
So much that I could do if I could just find the
time

[Bridge]
Lord don't let me be in such a hurry
Trying to live my life that I miss You in it
Help me to take the time to see
All that I need…

More Like You

Anonther song from my journey by
Kim Hill and Jamie Kenney

Your love overwhelms me
Your peace is beyond compare
Your mercy waits to surround me
If I dare
So I kneel before You, Father
In the shadow of Your might
And I pray that You will hear this cry
And heal my heart tonight

(Chorus)
I'm longing for You, Lord
I need You to fill me more and more
I'm desperate for You, Jesus
Whatever You have to do
Make me more like You

I've known You in my sorrow
I've seen You through my tears
I feel the warmth of Your touch
When You're near
May the scars I bear be sacred
And this brokenness be real
May the wounds so deep inside my heart
Reflect You as they heal

Strengthen me
According to your promise
Renew me
With the fragrance of your word
Hold me up, if the water overtakes me
That I may give you praise

The Feeling Wheel

Developed by Dr. Gloria Willcox
(just in case you need a cheat sheet)

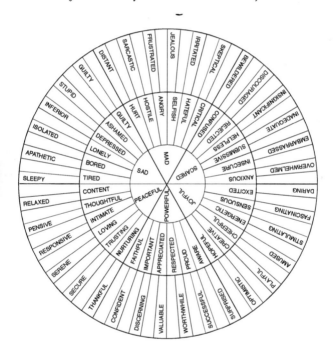

Beside Still Waters

During one of my sessions, my coach handed me a book that really hit home. It was entitled, ***The Worn Out Woman,*** by Dr. Steve Stephens and Alice Gray. I highly recommend it to any WOW out there. One of my favorite passages in the book is below:

There is a longing in my heart to come along side of all the (crazy busy women) of this world. If we could walk together for a while, I would share my regrets about pushing the limits for too many years. Friend to friend, we could talk about the value of listening to God and taking care of ourselves, or reserving more empty places on our calendars, of treasuring relationships more than accomplishments.

Our journey would take us along a quiet path and over a little stone bridge to an open meadow. Kicking off our shoes and lying back in the grass, our faces turned to the warm sun, we would softly recite together Psalm 23. As our duet reached the words,

He makes me to lie down in green pastures,
He leads me beside the still waters,
He restores my soul.

we would smile, knowing this is God's pleasure.
Just a typical day—full and purposeful, with time to spare
for eternity.

Just picturing it makes me smile...

Are you a Worn Out Woman (WOW)?

(from *The Worn Out Woman*)

____You get irritable or impatient over little things.

____You have a hard time getting sleep or staying asleep.

____You seem overly emotional.

____Your body sometimes feels so wound up that you can't relax

____You think, *If I can just get through this, then I'm going to do some of the things I really want to do.*

____You get frustrated at how forgetful you are.

____You are easily distracted, even from things you enjoy.

____Your friends say you are moody.

____You run out of energy before your day is done.

____You find it hard to make definite decisions or to stick to them once they are made.

____You get fed up when things take longer than you plan.

____You find yourself eating when you really

aren't hungry.

____You avoid spending time with family or friends because they just take too much energy.

____You feel like nothing sounds fun or exciting.

____You enjoy the adrenaline rush of last-minute deadlines.

____You are not working up to your normal ability.

____You find that worry distracts you from reaching your goals.

____You have trouble delegating tasks because you think you can do them better.

Score   Stress Level

1-6   Mild to moderate—be careful.

7-12   Serious—may need to make changes.

13-18   Severe—get help now!

My Highly Recommended List

Candle Watching Music

(All currently on my iPod mini)

A Pianostrings Tribute

featuring the Music of Josh Groban

Jim Brickman

Various Artists – Lifescapes Pure Relaxation

My Favorite Candle Watching Activities

Writing God

Listening to my iPod (see above)

Reading the Bible

Journaling

Just staring…

My Favorite Place to Buy
a Candle and a Couch

Pottery Barn

My Favorite Wake Up and Head Into Work Music

Blur: Music That Brings Focus
(Includes my favorite wake-up songs:
Life in My Day and More Like You)

My Favorite Place to Pamper Myself

Margot's Euro Spa, Birmingham, MI

My Ultimate Body, Mind and Fuel Stops
To get rid of pain

The Michigan Institute for Human Performance
(MIHP)

www.mihp.net

(please forgive the shameless self-promotion)

To get my head on straight

Access Christian Counseling

www.accesschristiancounsel.com

To get my body the nutrition it needs

Cindy Graves, Nutritional Consultant

www.shaklee.net/cindygraves

References

1. Holy Bible
   New International Version (NIV)
   Contemporary English Version
   (CEV)
   The Message

2. Henry Cloud, *Boundaries: When to Say Yes, When to Say No, To Take Control of Your Life* (Grand Rapids: Zondervan, 1992).

3. Drs. Ron and Nancy Rockey and Kay Kuzma *Belonging* (Nampa:Pacific Press, 1999)

4. Dr. Steve Stephens and Alice Gray, *The Worn Out Woman: When Your Life is Full and Your Spirit is Empty* (Sisters: Multnomah Publishers, 2004).

5. Ellen White, *Ministry of Healing* (Bolinas:Shelter, 1990)

6. Dr. Gloria Willcox
   P.O. Box 48363
   St. Petersburg, FL 33743

McLaughlin/Lander Publishing
A Division of
TriPLAYnar Technology, Inc.

Real People. Real Stories. Real Life.

Quick Order Form

Fax Orders: (586) 268-6948. Send this form.

Telephone Orders: (586) 268-6942. Have your credit card ready.

On-line Orders: www.lessonsfromthecouch.com

Postal Orders: ML Publishing
                      31500 Dequindre Rd.
                      Warren, MI 48092

Please send me more FREE information on:
Other books   Speaking/Seminars

Name:_____
Address:_____
City:_____State:____Zip:_____
Telephone:_____
Email:_____

Sales tax: Please add 6% for products shipped to MI addresses.

Shipping by air:
U.S.: $4.00 for first book and $2.00 for each additional product.
International: $9.00 for first book; $5.00 for each additional
product (estimate).

Payment: Check   Credit Card
Visa   Mastercard   AMEX
Card number:_____
Name on Card:_____Exp. Date:_____